Amazing Grace
The Flourishing Mind

Book Two - Compassion

Dear Rob

You have a big huge
heart and so much
love for people.
Love Gitta 😊 May 2010

Amazing Grace
The Flourishing Mind

Book Two

Compassion

A book of reflection and inner guidance

GITA BELLIN

Amazing Grace Series

Dedication

To my parents
William and Margaret
who gave me
Life!

This book is dedicated
to every act of
Compassion shown
to me in my Life.

Without these loving
kindnesses I could
not have had
the experiences needed
to write this book.

Compassion

is one of

the highest of all

attractor patterns.

Inspired by David R. Hawkins, M.D., Ph.D. book Power v Force page 115, observations on strong and weak attractor patterns.

Compassion

Disclaimer

This book is written as a simple guide to offer the reader the opportunity to reflect on their life and make positive choices. This book is not intended to be considered as a legal, medical, or any other professional service. This information within this book is not a substitute for professional advice.

Should the reader require or desire legal, medical, or other expert advice the services of a competent professional should be sought. The author, publisher, their employees and agents, are not liable for any damages arising from, or in connection with, the use of or reliance on, any information contained in this book.

Note from Gita Bellin

To the best of my knowledge all the thoughts in this book have come from words I have said in teaching sessions, thought about in quiet moments of meditation and known as truths in my own heart.

Over the years it has been my privilege to study with many great teachers, to read wonderful books and listen to inspiring and gifted friends and I have absorbed their thoughts deep inside my being. I have done my utmost to avoid infringing the copyright of any previous thinkers. Many thoughts are deeply ingrained in my soul and it is difficult to remember back over fifty years of travelling, to an original source. Should I have inadvertently used someone else's idea, I apologise and at the same time acknowledge the wisdom.

Where and Who is Great Mind? Maybe as we all embrace the Light with more and more intensity there are no boundaries on knowledge and my mind and the mind of another are just one great thought process. When I sat down to write this book it flowed out and I felt I was a recorder, a scribe for Truth to manifest. I trust that others feel this also, and know that the source is the same.

Copyright © 2009 by Gita Bellin
All rights reserved

ISBN: 1-4392-4302-6
ISBN-13: 9781439243022
Library of Congress Control Number: 2009905202

Foreword - John McFarlane

"I have had the enormous privilege of leading a Fortune Global 500 company and having been a member of the leadership team of others. Now when I look back on my 40-year career, my one recurring memory is not about our business and financial success, but the creation of a high energy organisation with an enlightened culture, achieved through the release of the previously untapped energy of thousands of people across many countries.

For most of my business life I applied only what I now regard as a technical approach, focused on markets, strategy marketing, finance, operations, and HR (a term I now regard as demeaning implying that people are simply resources to be used or shed) together with all the other well-trodden paths of traditional business. It wasn't until I became responsible for the company as a whole and faced with the enormous complexity and uncertainty of steering a path to long-term success that I realised that a company was much more than the sum of its inputs and outputs and its impact on society as a whole could be enormous.

Imagine the challenge of ensuring that all the people for whom I was now responsible, many of whom I would never meet, did the right things and did things right day in and day out on their own volition, now and well into the future well beyond my own time as leader. The real insight was that people mattered more than anything else in business, and if we could create an adventure for our people that was worthy of them investing their working lives in our journey. Sadly many leaders promise such an adventure yet many end as nightmares for the people involved.

We forget at our peril that it is people, their collective ability and energy, how they feel about working in the organisation, how passionate and engaged they are in its agenda and how they work together for a common purpose that makes a company great. After all, people today are searching for meaning in their lives, and how they can make their own unique contribution in their lifetimes. Could we really bring meaning to work and unleash the latent energy and potential in our people?

Articulating an inspirational vision therefore was important as a first step, as a company needs to stand for something beyond making money that acts as its centre of gravity that governs all its decisions - a higher or moral purpose to make a lasting contribution to society and therefore to all stakeholders, particularly its people.   Such a vision is necessary but not sufficient. We also needed to gain the hearts and minds of our people by building a bond of trust between us that would probably take many years to build, but seconds to destroy if we broke the bond.

Our investment in building trust began by providing our people with things they valued but didn't expect us to provide, without requiring anything in return, such as subsidised computers for their children at home, crèches near our major offices, an internal free market for jobs where applicants chose their bosses and an open environment where people could articulate their views or issues without censorship or adverse consequences. People had freedom but were expected to be accountable for their actions, and were evaluated in the round, rather than on their last mistake. The foundation of trust that ensued allowed us to move to a values-based approach across the whole enterprise where true freedom could be unleashed together with the energy that ensued.

In the process we had many critics and sceptics both internally and externally who waited for it all to go pear-shaped. It is all too easy to revert to the mean, and requires courage to be really different as it is uncharted territory. To be real, therefore, progress needs to be measured. Ultimately, the top 20 values in our firm were all positive values, we became the leaders in our industry globally in the Dow Jones Sustainability Index, and Fortune proclaimed us as being in the top 20 companies in the Fortune Global 500 for leadership, and the highest in our industry. I say this only to demonstrate that truly putting people first has tangible real-world consequences.

In recognition, I would pay tribute to a great number of people inside our company and externally who helped us in our journey and achievements. Gita was one of those. She helped us build the courage to take the path of being different.

Fairness requires us to postpone judgment on specific events and to take things in the round. So, in our search for freedom with accountability taking risks has consequences. We appoint people based on what they are good at, their strengths, not on what they are not good at, and help them succeed by matching the role to their strengths, avoiding exposure to situations that expose their weaknesses. While it is clearly important to get a sense of results achieved as well as how valuable a person is to the business in order to reward them fairly and advance those with the most talent, performance appraisal systems place insufficient emphasis on people's qualities, and too great a focus on areas for improvement which can be dispiriting.

Nothing in life or business is ever perfect or exactly as we expect. That is the nature of risk. If my own career is at all representative, business and society needs to find a much better balance between freedom and accountability. Allowing greater degrees of freedom with accountability requires us to recognise that circumstances will not always work out as we had hoped, and that people are human. When adverse things happen or when people make mistakes, whether things get better or worse, is often a function of how we respond. The best person to fix a problem is the one who is accountable for doing so and in many cases the person who allowed or caused it to happen in the first place. Resilience is an essential skill. It requires us to look through specific issues, Resilience requires us to create an environment where everyone is focused on solutions rather than consequences. Such looking beyond the issue at hand requires us to be compassionate in adverse circumstances as a catalyst for renewed hope.

Unfortunately, in my experience, compassion is exercised all too rarely in the business world, probably because its benefits are not well understood, When embraced appropriately, it can unleash a force that otherwise would lay dormant. Bringing greater compassion to bear requires greater understanding and insight. I'm therefore delighted that my dear friend Gita has had the courage, insight and determination to break the ice and write this important book, to help our understanding and to take a more caring and compassionate way forward."

Contents

Dedication

Compassion

Disclaimer

Foreword

Contents

Acknowledgements

Preface

Amazing Grace

Thoughts Developed from Book One – Reflections

Why the Title "Amazing Grace"

Compassion

Affirmation of Compassion

Reflections on Compassion

Opening the Heart – Guided Reflections on Compassion

Acknowledgements

To Guruji, for his great love and enormous acts of Compassion. I have learned and gained so much from observing his life, listening and absorbing his teachings and opening my heart to his demonstration of Universal Love.

To John McFarlane for agreeing to write the foreword to this book. I am grateful for his friendship, deep insight and wise counsel, his laughter, compassion and all the opportunities he gave me to understand the world of business and for embracing and embedding the power of Compassion within his Company.

To Helena Cornelius, for permission to use her artwork and Jodie Barne's inspired use of this artwork for the cover design.

To James Wild of Quiet Earth Publications for the use of his music as a background to the Guided Reflections on Compassion.

To Maureen Connor for supporting the creation of the manuscript and constantly reminding me to write this book – even to the point of putting a poster up in my office so I saw it everyday and in the end could delay no longer.

To Ruth Buckley, for checking the manuscript and preparing the layout for submission.

To Adrian Machon, Judy Malan and Karen Muller for their enthusiasm, encouragement and important suggestions for the improvement of the manuscript.

To Tracy Simpson and Alexia Miall, for their editing skills, friendship and belief in me and their enthusiastic support for this work.

Preface

This little book on Compassion is the second book in the
Amazing Grace series.

Twenty years have passed since the publication of Reflections -
Book One of the series.

The question is why?

Twenty years ago I realized that any deep reflective thoughts in
relation to comprehending Compassion required a state of
consciousness that had truly explored Compassion. Even now
at age 70 years I am only just beginning to comprehend the
multi-layered depths behind each of the thoughts in this book. It
is a challenge to have a vulnerable heart. We have all been
wounded at sometime or another. Our heart has experienced
attack and/or injury in many ways, especially that of a non-
physical nature. Our memories fear that the heart will be entered
into this way again. Even today as I open a page I understand
and realise something new about life. About my heart.
Thankfully I am grateful for that.

This continual exploration of my inner world keeps me young in
my heart and offers continuity of meaning and purpose to my life.

I have written some notes on my purpose for this book plus some
references to some of the individual thoughts on Compassion
which have particular meaning for me. In addition I felt it
important to include a few sections from the Amazing Grace
Book One Introduction which may offer a helpful background to
the series for those readers not familiar with Book One.

Gita Bellin
June 2009

Amazing Grace

Amazing Grace! How sweet the sound,
That God should so love me.
I once was lost, but now am found;
Was blind, but now I see.

'Twas Grace that taught my heart to fear,
And Grace my fears relieved,
How precious did that Grace appear
The hour I first believed.

Through many a danger, toils and snares
I have already come;
'Tis Grace hath brought me safe this far,
And Grace will lead me home.

The Lord has promised good to me,
His word my hope secures,
He will my shield and portion be,
As long as life endures.

And when this flesh and heart shall fail,
And mortal life shall cease,
I shall possess within the veil,
A life of joy and peace.

When we've been (thru) ten thousand years,
Bright shining as the sun,
We've no less days to sing God's praise
Than when we've first begun.

+++++++++++++

Newton 17th Century American Traditional

Thoughts Developed from Book One – Reflections

My first encounter with a little book of daily guidance and meditation was a channelled publication 'God Calling', (edited by A J Russell, published by Arthur James Ltd, UK). This was later followed by 'God at Eventide', (edited by A J Russell, published by Arthur James Ltd, UK). I was eight. The idea of producing several books of daily guidance each with a different focus and yet all connected, has been with me since that time.

The 'Amazing Grace' series is the result of a lifetime of personal spiritual searching, of persuading and cajoling by friends and colleagues, and innumerable letters and phone calls from friends and fellow travellers who have attended seminars I have taught, urging me to put into writing some of the thoughts and ideas I have gathered over the years. Many of the inclusions have been taken from typed transcripts of lectures I have given; others are from audio and video recordings, of those lectures. Some are contributions from notes taken by students in my classes. Others are just ideas that have come to me in quiet moments of meditation.

This book is meant to be a self teaching. The question of a teacher having the answer to our life is important because we can become dependent on that teacher. The Age of Pisces was an age of teachers, prophets and gurus. The Aquarian Age is an Age of Personal Sovereignty. I have been observing at the onset of this Age that the thrust for growth and knowledge is one of self sufficiency and sovereignty. The flashes of insight that come in the quietness of one's own being, the sudden knowing in the moment, are usually more permanent and profound than long hours of protracted study and discursive thinking. I feel this approach is an important learning for the 21st Century.

Before I began this book I asked myself if I were to own this book, why would I want it? How would I use it? What would I want to come to me when holding the yearning for growth in my mind? What kind of sayings would be needed to stimulate me into that 'Ah Ha' experience? The inclusions are the result of these questions.

2

As a teacher I have been teaching this knowledge for years. How many teachers truly live their truth? I certainly have not. Perhaps in part. So I made the choice that I would write the book to teach me. Teachers only teach in order to learn, and I must be my most resistant pupil. And after all, who teaches whom? Publication is for me a sharing of talents and that gives meaning to my individual gifts and brings me closer to the world of 'Love in Action.' Many friends and students have told me that my off hand remarks have challenged them to move through their self imposed boundaries. For this reason I have included some challenging sayings in this book which may not be comfortable but will certainly be truthful.

And so I present this little book of thoughts on Compassion, which over the years has inspired me to continually ask questions and find answers.

How to use this Book

In moments of silence, contemplation and prayer, before or after meditation, in moments of confusion and loss, simply surrender to the Force of Love - That Amazing Grace - within and without, and the answer is there. You will be amazed at how much you know. The Spirit within always knows the answer, it's just our limited self that forgets that life's challenges are opportunities. In times of intense human experience, if you are like me, we need constant reminding that this experience of life is an awe inspiring, brilliant creation for growth.

Approach this book as if you were looking in a mirror – for you are one to yourself. Book in hand, find a quiet moment, a place in Nature, a nice comfortable armchair, take a deep breath, feel the depth of Silent Being in your soul, and ask yourself for your answer.

With gentle reverence, for you are exposing yourself to yourself and this can be a very vulnerable experience, open the book. There on the page and deep within the interpretation of the

3

words will be your answer. Even if you do not think it so! This little book is simply a reminder of what you already know. Give yourself the gift of exploring all avenues of your knowing. Enjoy!

Thank you for owning the book. Each expanded thought as a result of its use is an ever widening ripple in the Ocean of Love. I salute the Divinity within you and within me that draws us together through the experience.

Why the Title 'Amazing Grace.'

Why the title 'Amazing Grace?' I have observed in my growth pattern over my life span that when I want to sincerely know, the knowledge comes from the most unexpected and spontaneous sources. Browsing in a book shop or a library, turning the car radio on to a programme I never usually tune into, a chance meeting with a friend or stranger. There is the answer that I have been searching for. There must be something working to create these awe inspiring moments of miracle. The natural wondrous discovery of life which I had as a child and I am learning to reclaim.

All my life, in whatever circumstances I have found myself, I have felt protected. Call this protection, God, the Light, the God Force, my Guides, a Being of Light protecting and guiding me. It has always been there and it has never failed me. I have always felt an unseen presence. The innumerable times in life that I have reached out for a sign, a direction to turn towards, a support to give strength, this unseen Grace has never failed me. I suppose you could say that I have always trusted this Force never to let me down. I feel this Force as a Father/Mother presence. Later I intellectualised that it is in me as well as around me in everything else.

Thus I came to comprehend that Love's only true purpose is to re-unite with Love. When I feel separate from Love it is only a feeling of isolation in me and so I gently surrender to the flow of life in Love, release my fear, my anxiety, my apprehension and guided by the Grace of Love, I reach out for that point of union.

4

It comes in many ways, the smile of a friend, a spontaneous circumstance in my life, words that uplift me in a moment, the cry of a bird, the joy of sunset, the smell of rain on earth. They give me the ease to let go, to feel the inner flash of illumination, the 'Ah yes, of course!' Then I know that is It. A sweet silence reunites me with the 'Peace that Passeth All Understanding'.

For me the words of the book title embrace the form and the energy of the whole intention for the book being in being. Every time it is touched, glanced at, opened and studied the reader can be embraced, surrounded and uplifted by the energy of the form. This energy then uplifts and expands the sincerity of the soul search. In fact a miracle can occur. In choosing the title I trusted the reader to know that this is a powerful intention. Dictionaries are wonderful books. They show the heritage of words and teach us to observe the soul of man striving to find ways of communicating the exploration of his being. Should you turn to the word 'Grace' you will find such descriptions as, 'becomingness', 'beauty in action', 'an instance of favour', 'favour in manifestation', 'an exceptional privilege', thanksgiving', 'the conferring of honour and dignity', 'to gratify and delight'. The word 'Amaze" or 'Amazing' is just as uplifting. Descriptions such as 'to astound and awe', 'to overwhelm with wonder', 'great beyond expectation', 'wonderful'.

Do we not deserve this for ourselves! In transition from childhood to adulthood we forget what a wondrous, free flowing, spontaneous fun loving child there is inside. We have, as humanity, forgotten our birthright as the Light.

Just for a moment sit and hold this book, ask in the sincerity of your heart for the answer to life's current exciting opportunity for growth and feel yourself surrounded by Grace. Confer upon yourself honour and dignity, knowing who you truly are and that you always knew. Experience the exceptional privilege of you teaching you. Feel the power of your manifestation and the favour you are granting yourself out of this moment of truth, where, surrounded by beauty in action and exceptional privilege, you delight yourself in the knowledge that you know and all you need to know is there inside. And give thanks.   Gita Bellin

Compassion

There is no simple definition of Compassion. The Oxford Dictionary states that it is – "suffering with another – a fellow feeling". The dictionary also states it is "pity that inclines one to spare or succour".

For me these definitions belong to a past age. Suffering and pity have a great historical history for many and are valid experiences. However there is a state of Compassion that is different. It is a state of the Evolved Heart and an Evolved Life where Compassion is a state of unification rather than one of separation.

I have learnt during my 70 years that Compassion is about my unique response to life choices.

For me it is the measure of my Compassion in any situation related to the mastery of the choice I make between a reactive response to life or a creative response to life. Everyone expresses their Compassion in various degrees through their choice of conduct. Reaction always causes polarity - separateness - whereas creation offers the opportunity for heartfelt connection and aliveness.

In all our responses it is possible to discover specific qualities of thought, feeling and emotion which enable a State of Compassion to be present. When in a state of Compassion the heart is able to stay open without risk and constriction. The important and challenging thought is "without risk".

We cannot **do** Compassion.

We can only **be** Compassion.

In programs where I have taught that **Compassion is a way of Being**, many have explored this concept with me. Gradually over the last twenty years the following points have emerged.

6

Compassion

A state of the heart.

In Compassion the heart is able to stay open without risk or constriction.

Compassion is a state of empathy with the heart.

A State of Compassion views the world, and is in the world, from a place of Self.

Compassion enables a state of dignity and honour regarding the individual life journey.

Compassion enables the individual to honour their own and another's pain.

Compassion enables the whole person to be present.

Let us explore Compassion more deeply. The dictionary definition of Compassion is: "to feel with another".

It also states in the dictionary that "it is a form of love in expression to someone else", "where the purpose is to see that (someone else) becomes strong and independent" *and free of fear* (my addition). In this way Compassion unites people with a deep sense of feeling.

Given the level of fear in the world and particularly in the old hierarchical structures of the 20th Century, Compassion needs to be explored and demonstrated. When we assist someone through a barrier whether it be with creativity, difficulties with families, difficulties with work colleagues, difficulties with a skill or simply anxiety or fear about a situation, we are letting go of fear. When this assistance is given **freely** with love, that is an act of Compassion.

There is a difference between Compassion and Sympathy

Sympathy is where we commiserate with another. How often have we, over coffee, agreed with a friend or colleague how bad the other person is in the story that is being told. Compassion is different. It is where we reach out a hand and in kindness offer creative opportunities without judgment or blame.

The purpose of embracing Compassion is to be empowered, independent and free of fear.

Non-judgment is the key

The embracing of Compassion as a state assists us to understand how the personality we have can fulfill our life purpose. The ego can be transformed. It is never destroyed. Energy can be transformed into a higher state. Nothing dies. Everything is eternal. Even the illusion of our perception of reality when transformed, becomes a new temporary reality, until the next step of life is worked through, and we experience a new level of perception and truth.

The power and strength of our individual personality is the quality we require and need at various stages of our life, in order for us to become the person we were meant to be. These qualities are needed to fill our hearts and minds with the necessary attributes to stand alone at times, upon our path, and speak our truth.

This power of personality when functioning from a greater depth can be balanced or unbalanced. When unbalanced, the individual gives offence and takes offence and thus adds negativity to the world. When balanced, the individual takes love and gives love and adds love and light to the world.

When there is passion to live our lives from the standpoint of accountability, we embrace the important element of Compassion. Compassion is more than just love. It is vital to allow thoughts without attachment to motivate our actions; then our emotions will not have charge to provide impetus and our feelings will be experienced without being distorted. Then we will

8

definitely draw to ourselves only those events in life that will meet our unfulfilled needs and eventually assist us to do the work that is our destiny to fulfill.

Imbalance occurs when the ego is destroyed. For without the individual personality, we become passive, joyless, ineffective and pale as a human being. It is this misunderstanding that has caused people to become ineffective in the past. Imbalance can also occur when the ego is empowered and gives rise to greed, control, destruction and personal survival, at the expense of others. Between these two is the point of the truth of Compassion.

It is our birthright to live and acknowledge our specialness, our uniqueness, our contribution to life, not because we need others to recognise it, but simply because it is real. Every individual carries a special gift. Once it is recognised we can choose to demonstrate it when circumstances call upon us to do so.

Throughout history, singular people have made a difference and have discovered truths that have changed and transformed society forever. These people have spoken truths that have been recorded and remembered for future generations.

Yes, our world has patches of darkness. However, we all have the ability to constantly add positivity to the world. Each one of us has the power and capacity to reach deep down within ourselves and take that creative power of Compassion and transform our world and transform our reality into what we would wish for our children and grandchildren.

Each one of us can make a difference – one smile, one well spoken word, one gesture, one act of kindness, one piece of guidance given – all these things have made a difference in the past and can make a difference in the future. When we, several individuals, many singular people, work together, knowing that we can transform our lives, we will affect the lives of all those who come in contact with us. When we are constant in our belief that we make a difference in every moment, then all the shadowy places – all the conflicts in our lives and the lives of those that we are in relationship with – will begin to ease.

Freedom means the rights of all ones. However, with that right comes a deeper sense of responsibility for that which we are and that which we create. Freedom means not interfering with the choices of others and, at the same time, uplifting them to greater demonstrations of individual uniqueness.

Freedom means freedom from judgment. Freedom from that which binds and holds one back. Freedom from misconception. Freedom from anything that is not in complete resonance and harmony.

We are all facing challenging times. Our mindsets are changing. Our previous thought patterns are being challenged and this can make us feel uncomfortable and unsure. All this is simply moving us from being consciously unskilled into being consciously skilled in relation to Compassion. All this is meant to empower us. Mindsets (belief systems) are given to us as a tool for our minds to help us come ever closer to something which is so vast that it cannot, of itself, ever be fully contained within any one belief system. So, our belief systems only give us a partial aspect of truth and thus our life becomes an exploration and an adventure into truth.

True knowledge, which is the ultimate wisdom, comes from within the heart. What emerges is a resonance – a knowing – which is beyond all words and which is the ultimate expression of our spirit within.

It is through Compassion that we are asked to demonstrate our mastery. Every day, we are given the opportunity to master our thoughts and feelings – to be truly creative with the adventure called life. How we respond to the adventure demonstrates our level of the mastery of Compassion.

The individual thoughts that follow offer opportunities to expand these necessary attributes, in order for Compassion to become a powerful force in our life. They relate to all points covered in this discussion of Compassion. Some develop over two or more pages. Do not rush the process. Allow the flow of realisation to come forth.   Gita Bellin

10

Compassion

Note: There is no punctuation in some of the reflections on Compassion. This has a purpose.

Affirmation of Compassion

All of my life experiences
are a blessing.

They have taken me
through the school
called Life.

*In every moment I am
offered the opportunity to
transcend polarity*

*And return Home
Whole
In Grace*

Realisations

are the

Integration

Of

Knowing

We cannot

do

Compassion.

We can only

be

Compassion.

Compassion

is an endless state

of Love.

Without Compassion

this planet

will always be

a battlefield.

Wake up!

Wake up!

Unhappy voices

Call out from

Everywhere.

The Inevitable step
for humanity
in the 21st Century

COMPASSION NOW

Choice
is of the heart.

Select freely
after consideration.

This transcends
right and wrong,
good and bad.

We are released
from blame, shame
and doubt.

Decision
is of the rational mind.

When we decide
we are at the
effect of reason.

We make the
alternative wrong.

Seek Meaning.

Meaning emerges
Purpose.

Purpose provides
Answers.

*Compassion
requires us
to honour
another's pain.*

*What do we know
of their life journey,
their trauma,
the unkindnesses,
the hurts,
done to them.*

Unfeeling
we sit before
the evening news.

Do we allow
our heart to connect.

To send a prayer,
a thought of love,
to the faces
on the screen,
of our Life?

Is it easier to ignore
another's pain?

What would it take
to feel and know
another's pain,
another's hunger,
another's mutilation,
another's loss through war,
another's hopelessness,
another's helplessness,
another's contemplation
of suicide?

Compassion
is simply
the consequence
of the choices
we make.

Compassion

has

no Polarity

Ease

someone's

pain

today,

including your own.

Accept all

life's challenges

as the

Realisation of Dreams.

When we own
that every experience
is an opportunity
to master life,

we gain Compassion
for ourself
and Compassion
for others.

Every challenge

of the heart

is an opportunity

for

Transformation.

Illuminated Leadership

requires the

core presence

of

Compassion.

Compassion,

Positive thinking

prolongs life.

Fear

blocks life.

Intuition
is a gift of
Compassion

from the Heart.

Accept Fully

your Heartfelt Ability

to know.

Connect your
Mind - Heart - Soul
into the current
situation of difficulty.

Ask what the Heart
knows.

Ask what the Soul
needs.

Ask what the Mind
chooses.

Surrender to the Heart.

The Heart knows what the Intellect does not.

When we fully
comprehend
the wondrous
inter-relationship
of all form,

we move into a
State of Compassion.

Rest for a Moment

be still

reflect

move through the door
of confusion

into a Future.

How can we lead

others to find

Compassion

if we have not

found it ourself

Judgment
creates distance.

Separation.

No Room! No Room!

Compassion cries,
and Dies.

Observe the bee
and the open flower.

Would that my heart
could be so open
for every stranger.

*Compassion
gives us the ability
to view life
through the purity
of What Is.*

*Judgment opposes
the purity
of the experience
of Life.*

The mystery

of our life

opens up

when we begin

to know

the heart.

In the moment
when Compassion exists
these qualities are present.

Purity
Innocence
Awareness
Beauty
Love
Kindness
Placement
Attention
Grace

Compassion

is a purr

with closed eyes.

Compassion

is

a wagging tail.

Every tear,

Every fear,

is a

thousand years.

Be Kind

Every Communication
reveals truths about

our Beliefs
our Thoughts
our Feelings
our Values
our Priorities
our Needs
our Purpose
our Meaning

The Secret of Life
reveals Itself
in every moment.

Be Grateful

Trust requires

a state of

Compassion.

What is important

is invisible

to the eye.

The Heart

is the key.

In a State

of Compassion

False Identities

fall away.

*Never ever
miss a moment
to transmit
Love.*

*As a Thought
As a Word
As a Smile
As a Prayer*

Self Respect

is the discipline

to say

NO

to your limited self.

Empowerment without

Compassion

is not

Empowerment.

Notice the people

your Heart

has called into

your Life.

Panic annihilates

Love and Compassion.

Stop

Feel

Breathe

Act

Everything

is Love.

With bare feet

stand

on Mother Earth.

Connect

with all Life.

Be bold

Be different

Be courageous

Be known

Be visionary

Embrace Compassion

Look

See silence,

wrapping the leaf,

cradling the raindrop,

receiving a sunbeam.

Know

Divine Compassion

Exists

Intention

stabilises Attention.

Intention

provides Willingness.

Situations are ever

significant.

This situation

is a gift.

Attention

effects perception.

Pay Attention

to everything.

Feed

your

Soul

Realisations

are

the Integration

of

Knowing

In every Moment

Experience is being

called forth

into Wisdom.

Progression through

the lows and the highs

of Life

strengthens the Heart.

The highest form
of Compassion
is the expression
of a human being
in a state of love
with all Life
Everywhere.

We ARE

Universal Beings

Intimacy in Relationship

is the

co-creation of a

Great Work.

It unfolds

in the Moment.

Never ever give up

*A life lived
from the standpoint
of accountability
embraces
the important element
of Compassion.*

The writing
of a life
never ends.

Through our children
we simply
pass on the pen.

When ready
they write
their story.

Our Words,
our Compassion,
our Way of Being,

inspires others
to live
their dreams.

Trust yourself.

Trust your process
and
look for signs
of Spring.

Giving heed

creates the opportunity

for Compassion to

Manifest and Become.

Our story

is

our Legacy

Compassion

fits perfectly

into our Life.

Our Life

is unique.

Seek Silence.

Find the meaning

in the moment.

The Noble Heart

sighs

with Realisation.

Reflect

Trust

Forgive

Know

Be

I am the Candle.

You are the Match.

You are the Candle.

I am the Match.

Compassion is the

Flame and the Light.

Together.

We are the Candle.

We are the Match.

We are the Flame.

We are the Light.

Who am I?

*How am I
living my Life?*

The Essence of

the

Spiritual Life

is

Compassion

Be satisfied.

Use your gifts

with Gratitude.

Share with Everyone.

We cannot hide

from

Knowing.

Knowing

is Trust

deep within

the Heart.

It is impossible

to be in a continuous

State of Compassion

without the ability

to be in

Trans-Egoic

Witness Consciousness.

Begin the day

Breathe in the wind

Compassion flows

Compassion.

A state of

Active

Silent

Safety.

Be aware when
places and people
are silent.

Much is happening.

Silence is Loud.

The illusion is that

Busy-ness is safe.

Silence is safer.

Why fear Silence

Soul and Psyche.

Spirit and Personality.

A miraculous handclasp

of

immeasurable

potential possibility.

Through that wondrous gap
where
Awareness is aware
of Awareness.

Compassion trickles in.

Compassion seeps through
into
Conscious Awareness.

Love

is not what

people say.

It is what

they do.

Every parent
begins with the
Absolute Resolution
to place their child
in their Heart.

What is Love?

A leaf on a tree

A petal on a flower

A fly lost

on a window pane.

What is easier to Love?

Judgment

pre-supposes attachment

to right and wrong.

Non attachment to outcome

offers the opportunity

for a true Creative Act.

A true Creative Act
is
Discontinuous with History.

Compassion is a

true Creative Act.

Why bother to be

mediocre.

Nothing is Half way.

Everything is Whole way.

Everything

is the Way.

In the process of Life

do we trust

Divine Timing

for things to be

the way they are?

Is IT
as
IT is?

If innocence is
not present,
how can we Be
in the moment?

Become Aware
that this moment
has a freshness
that has never
happened before
in the Eternity of Time.

Compassion is choice
in the moment.

Exchange Restriction

for

Freedom.

Laugh

at

yourself.

*Do I do
those things,
expected of me?*

*Do I do
those things,
my Spirit
requires me
to do?*

Embrace Compassion

as an act of

Service

and the

Heroic Journey

of Choice.

Non threatening people
are safe for others
to seek out.

We set a field
of Compassion
where people gravitate
towards us.

When all behaviour
is seen as an
Expression of Love

We are Free
to Serve
in a special way.

Adopt an old person.

Bake cookies.

Visit.

Share Wisdom.

Compassion

is born into

Everyone.

It is an

Eternal Quality.

Self sabotage

denies

the Heart.

When Compassion
is present.

Our anxieties
and our dreams
bring us together.

Belief is of the
Intellect.
It can be shattered
by doubt
at any time.

Choice is of the
Heart.

It is energetic.
It is a
Divine Force.

When we embody
and live
anything,

We become it.

Growth does not
need to increase
separateness.

Compassion creates
the movement
to bring others
with us.

Emotional Charge
is a
great challenge.

When an emotion
is charged
it creates polarity.

We can choose to
stop the charge
at any time.

A life without

Compassion

impoverishes

the Heart.

Compassion

is the oldest

Spiritual knowledge

of our Planet.

It has its roots

in all Creation

and lost Civilisations.

Compassion

simply

IS

Judgment

not hate

Is the opposite

to Love.

In a state of Compassion,
the state of Relatedness,
becomes the operating
principle for the
21ˢᵗ Century.

Guided Reflection on Compassion

A recording of a guided Compassion exercise has been created. It offers the listener an opportunity to work with the exploration of the depth of Compassion required for Opening the Heart.

Compassion is explored through many layers of experience. The subtleties of the depth of the Heart are revealed. With gentle relaxing music as a background, Gita leads the listener into the depths of the Heart.

This Compassion process is used in much the same way as the experience offered in the Leaders for Change and Advanced Personal Mastery workshops that she has taught over many decades.

The content of the recording is as follows:

Track 1   A short introduction and instructions for the
               process

Track 2   Exploring the depth of the Heart
               Letting go of the hurts of the Heart
               Embracing a renewed vibrancy of Compassion
               Embedding this new vibrancy of Compassion

The music used as a background to the spoken voice has been specially created for healing meditation and reflection. The music chosen is "Spirit Traveller".

The Compassion recording and the original music "Spirit Traveller" by James Wild are available as downloads at www.quietearth.org

Email chris@quietearth.org

Note from Gita: For me the book is incomplete without the recorded exercise. I therefore greatly encourage the reader to obtain the recording. The experience of the process of opening the heart, healing the heart and letting go, has proved to be life transforming to the many people who have attended the Advanced Personal Mastery Seminar.

About the Author

Gita Bellin has long been acknowledged as one of the pioneers of the Behavioural Transformation Revolution in human performance, cultural transformation and spiritual awareness.

Since 1965 she has taught personal growth, stress management, cultural change and meditation programs throughout the world. Following an early career in English Universities, she travelled through Europe, Greece, Turkey, Iran, Afghanistan, Pakistan and India, seeking for answers. Many of the answers that she discovered are in her Amazing Grace Series of books.

For 10 years Gita has been an advisor to one of the world's largest consulting firms. She has trained Consultants and Facilitators to deliver cultural and behavioural change programs. Her work is now offered on all continents in many languages throughout the world.

Gita has spent almost fifty years studying and teaching the knowledge and philosophies of Eastern and Western disciplines, behavioural and spiritual. She has been trained in a range of advanced spiritual practices for 12 years with her first teacher and 17 years with her second teacher.

Gita lives on a farm surrounded by people, cows, kangaroos, wombats, chooks, eagles, parrots, cockatoos, kookaburras and her favourite person, Meggsie the Cat.

It is her sanctuary since much of her time is spent travelling the world inspiring individuals, groups and corporations to transform the quality of their lives.

Gita continues to offer a full range of personal growth, behavioural and cultural change, stress management and facilitator development programmes. Professionally she is presently offering all her programmes through Performance Consultants International.

This little book is a response to all fellow travellers seen and unseen on the path to joy. So many people have urged me for so long to publish a daily guide on Compassion related to a variety of circumstances. This guide is intended to be a reminder that we constantly create the most wonderful and awe inspiring array of opportunities and life lessons as we journey along our way.

Our spirit within always knows the answer; it is just our limited self that forgets that life's challenges are opportunities. In times of intense human experience, if you are like me, we need constant reminding that the experience of life is an awe inspiring, brilliant creation for growth. Book in hand find a quiet place in Nature, a comfortable armchair or a soft warm bed. Take a deep breath, feel the depth of the soul within, and ask yourself for the answer. With gentle reverence, for you are exposing self to Self, and this can be a very vulnerable experience, open the book. There will be your answer, even if you do not think so. Give yourself the gift of exploring all avenues of your knowing.

Other books in the Amazing Grace Series include

- ***Reflections – Book 1***
- ***Forgiveness – Book 3***

Nine other books are in progress.

For information regarding all open courses for the public, as well as in-house and tailored courses in organisations, including Leadership Development Programmes and Facilitator Development Programmes, designed and delivered by Gita Bellin, please contact:

David Brown, Chief Executive Officer
Performance Consultants International

Direct: +44 (0)792 1360 343
Office: +44 (0)207 3736 431

Email: davidbrown@performanceconsultants.com

Website: www.performanceconsultants.com

Notes

Notes

Notes

Notes

Made in the USA
Charleston, SC
25 February 2010